SOUTHWOLD
IN
OLD POSTCARDS

D1382007

Richard Frost

Thomas Moulton Publications

i

This edition published by Thomas Moulton Publications
76 Stradbroke Road
Southwold
Suffolk
IP18 6LQ

ISBN 0-9543817-0-X

Printed and bound in Great Britain by Micropress
27 Norwich Road
Halesworth
Suffolk
IP19 8BX

To Ann

CONTENTS

INTRODUCTION

The idea to try and compile a book about Southwold from old postcards brings together in one project two compelling interests of mine both at the same time and in a way at the same place. Southwold never ceases to beguile residents and visitors alike. I have to confess I have long since fallen victim to its many charms and the collecting of old postcards, especially of the town as it used to be, is a hobby that has captured and held my attention unlike anything else for a great number of years.

Having collected all manner of objects at different times during my life, my fascination with the humble postcard has been my most enduring interest and probably needs some explanation.

Postcards in their quiet and usually understated way have the unique ability to whisk you back in time to a different era. The places, people and events that are captured by the camera or artist give a tantalising glimpse of life as it used to be, making the postcard a significant historical resource. Sometimes as a bonus the sender may have added a message on the back which brings an intensely personal dimension to such an unassuming artifact.

The Post Office Act of 1870 permitted the use of postcards for the first time and in 1894 picture postcards in the squarish format of the Court Card began to appear. It was not until 1899 when the Post Office adopted the internationally accepted standard size and format that they became popular. In 1902 Britain became the first country to allow senders of postcards to write on the same side as the address. After this, postcards were sent in their millions and collecting them became a national craze.

Although the postcard has been in use for over a century it is generally agreed that the Golden Age of the Postcard was between the years of 1902 - 1914. At that time they were regarded as the cheapest and also one of the most reliable means of communication in an age before telephones became widely available.

If you are seeking the vernacular of Southwold the postcard is where you will find it. Few things in and about Southwold, whether places, events or even people, have not ended up at some stage as the subject of a postcard. Those early visitors to Southwold at the turn of the last century, many of them arriving on the Southwold Railway (itself the subject of numerous post-cards), bought and sent postcards home to family and friends. What they chose depended on what they found interesting or appealing about the town and was available as the subject of a postcard. Postcard publishers both national and local were quick to capitalise on the sheer volume of photographic opportunities the town provided for postcards as well as the ready market for their products among a population swollen by summer visitors.

Southwold was fortunate in this respect to have its very own photographer and publisher in Frederick Jenkins who arrived in the town at the beginning of the last century and set up his shop in High Street opposite Barclays Bank. For the next fifty or so years Frederick Jenkins captured on film just about every facet of life in Southwold at every opportunity. He was an astute business man as his advertisements of the time proclaimed that he had well over 200 different cards to choose from at his shop, including views, churches, fishermen, events "and everything of interest."

IS IT WISE

To buy Postcards from a man who can only show you an assortment of 18 or 20 different views, when by going to

F. Jenkins

92 and 94, High Street, SOUTHWOLD,

you can have over

200 *different Local Postcards*

to select from ?

---

45 different Black and White Postcards   10 for **6d.**

30 different Coloured Postcards
           (18 *being reproduced from paintings*).

12 Coloured Postcards in packet   -   -   **6½d.**

6 " Oilette " Postcards -   -   -   -   **6d.**

6 " Sylvester Stannard " Postcards   -   -   **9d.**

6 Walberswick Postcards   -   -   -   **6d.**

The **30** *Coloured Postcards, post free, for* **2/4.**

---

6 " Punch " Local Postcards   -   -   6 for **6d.**

3 Geographical Postcards   -   -   **1d.** each

---

130 *Photographic Postcards,*

Including **VIEWS, LOCAL CHURCHES, FISHERMEN, EVENTS,** and everything of interest.   Price **2d.** each.

Postage extra for all Postcards.

29

I have no idea what the full extent of his portfolio might have looked like as Jenkins unfortunately did not number any of his cards but his prolific output serves to provide a unique and lasting legacy of the town and its inhabitants. Of the cards I have selected on the following pages there are many which were produced by Frederick Jenkins but I have used cards from other publishers as well, to provide further insight and balance to the project. The cards have been grouped according to their geographic location so that the reader may travel in a circular route from the pier, along the beach to the harbour and then back across the common and through the town, to finish once again in the vicinity of the pier.

I have had by necessity to be selective in my choice of postcards, all of which come from my own personal collection and acknowledge that the ones I have chosen represent a personal choice rather than a fully comprehensive view of the subject. I trust that readers will understand this and that hopefully it will in no way diminish their enjoyment of the book as it is presented.

It is among my hopes that this book will bring back memories for those who knew the town as it once was and for others, that it will introduce them to a town and a time in history when the pace of life was much slower than it is today.

Above all I hope that this book will provide the sort of pleasure to readers that I have experienced in compiling it.

Richard Frost   Southwold   September 2002

THE PROSPECT

Aerial View of Southwold

Publisher unknown and not postally used.

Major landmarks such as the church, pier and lighthouse are easily recognisable. There are marshes and part of the Common to be seen in the foreground and with closer inspection the outlines of South Green and Gun Hill should be discernible. Southwold House is also prominent in the foreground and the octagonal building known as the Casino may be seen on Gun Hill.

Southwold is virtually an island bounded on the east by the North Sea on the south and west by the river Blyth and on the north west and west by Buss Creek. Altogether the area enclosed by these boundaries amounts to about one square mile.

The town itself is situated on a low gravel hill sufficiently elevated to give commanding views out to sea as well as much admired panoramic views from the Common, towards Walberswick to the south and Blythburgh to the west. To the north of the town there are uninterrupted views across the marshes towards Easton Bavents and Covehithe.

Bird's Eye View Of Southwold

Bird's Eye View of Southwold

Publisher unknown. Postally used on 27th August 1923.

Horace writes to Miss Chamberlain in Portslade "Having a fine time, am spending the day here. With love and kisses."

This postcard was taken from the top of the water tower on the Common and gives a fine view of the houses along Godyll Road. The church and lighthouse are easily discernible in the distance and the chimney of Adnams brewery may also be seen above the roofscape. The entrance to York Road is gated off and cattle are roaming freely on the Common with not a car in sight!

ALONG THE BEACH

The Pier

Appears to have been taken from a window in the Grand Hotel and shows virtually the full length of the Pier with a "Belle" steamer approaching the T-end. Notice the bathing machines on the beach. This card was published by F. Jenkins and postally used on April 22nd 1905.

G.R.B. writes to Miss. I. Balcombe "Weather here is cold and bleak."

The Southwold Pier Order was approved by Parliament in 1899 and work started almost immediately. On October 2nd 1899 the first wooden pile was driven in. The head was reached on March 7th 1900 and the pier opened for business in the June of that year.

It was built by the Coast Development Company, which had purchased approximately 20 acres of land known as the Town Farm Estate from the Borough for £8,000 in 1897. A promise was made at the time to build a pier within three years. The structure was designed by W. Jaffrey M. I. C. E. and the contract for construction was awarded to Anthony Fasey and Sons, Leytonstone. When finished it extended to approximately 810 feet, was 26 feet wide with a T-end 120 feet by 30 feet. It was 12 feet above high water. The total cost of the undertaking was £8,000.

The pier was a strictly commercial venture in that it was designed to act primarily as a landing stage for the Belle Steamers that plied the East Coast at the time, bringing to Southwold holidaymakers from London as well as day trippers from places like Yarmouth and Lowestoft. On the evening of June 2nd 1900 the first steamer called at the pier amid much excitement and huge crowds. After this a regular timetable was quickly established with steamers arriving daily from Great Yarmouth at 11.00 a.m. and from London at about 6.00 p.m. during the season.

A single admission to the pier was 1d and a weekly ticket was 1/=.

In 1906 the Coast Development Company was wound up and ownership of the pier then passed to the Wembley Amusement and Equipment Company. By 1928 the Belle Steamer service too had ended and six years later the head of the pier was washed away in a storm. The commercial focus of the enterprise then moved more towards the shoreward end of what was left of the pier and into the world of entertainment. Many famous performers including Elsie and Doris Waters appeared on the stage in the pier pavilion. In 1936 the original pier pavilion was replaced with the two-storeyed building which still stands today.

After the outbreak of the Second World War it was felt necessary to section it some time in 1940 when there were real fears of an imminent German invasion along the East Coast. Later it was struck and damaged by a drifting sea mine. It was repaired after the war in 1948 at a cost of £30,000 but by now age was beginning to tell. It was severely damaged by a storm in October 1955 and the seaward end was again left isolated. A further gale in 1979 reduced the pier's length to little more than 90 feet so that it barely reached the water's edge.

The Iredale family is now the owner of Southwold pier. At the time of its purchase in 1987 it was in a much run down and neglected state. Rebuilding the pier began in 1999 with an E. E. C. grant helping towards a total cost estimated at £1,000,000, two thirds of which has been found by the family itself. Brian Haward, a local architect, has been responsible for the design of the new pier and the structural engineering involved has been undertaken by The Morton Partnership another local firm. The length of the reconstructed pier is 623 feet.

The pier was opened officially by the Duke of Gloucester on 3rd July 2001.

The Pier Approach

Pier and Approach, Southwold   66519 J.V

Published by Valentines in their XL series. It has not been postally used.

It shows the original timber pier pavilion with a hipped roof before it was replaced in 1936 with the present building.

Southwold Pier 1953

Publisher unknown. Not postally used.

This postcard shows the state of the pier battered and forlorn after the East Coast floods of February 1953.

Footnote : Sea Angling On Southwold Pier

Owing to the ease and comfort of fishing from the pier the sport became increasingly popular with flounders, codling, whiting, dabs, soles and conger eels being taken in abundance during the first season. Autumn and winter were considered the best times to catch fish.

Anglers were advised to use a rod with a "stiff end joint" and the preferred baits for cod and whiting were fresh herrings sliced open and cut into half-inch strips or sprats cut into four or five sections. Lugworms were also highly regarded as bait.

The first silver medal competition held on the pier was sponsored by Mr. R. J. Canova who was a local watchmaker, jeweller and silversmith as well as an enthusiastic fisherman. It was held over four consecutive Wednesday afternoons during December 1900 and was won by Mr. R. J. Walls with a weight of 9lb 8oz. of fish.

Perhaps one of the most unusual catches on the pier was that of Mr. J. Powditch landlord of the Sole Bay Inn who was fishing on Thursday Sept 24th 1907 when he caught a Skua gull.

Skuas are native to the Shetland Isles and rarely come this far south. They are by nature aggressive often chasing other sea birds and forcing them to give up the prey they have caught, but they will scavenge on all types of refuse found on sea or shore when the opportunity arises. This one apparently flew onto the pier and seized some fish when Mr. Powditch pounced. The captured bird was then exhibited at the Sole Bay Inn and was said in the report of the incident in the local paper "to be plump and in fine condition."

Southwold Belle

Published by H. Good. Not postally used.

The "Southwold Belle" was built for the Coast Development Company by William Denny & Bros. at Dumbarton and was launched in May 1900. She was the largest of the Belle Steamers at 535 gross tons and also the last to join the fleet operated by the Coast Development Company. She was in service between 1900 and 1911 bringing holiday - makers from London to and from the East Coast resorts as well as to her namesake port. During this time the paddle steamers were finding it increasingly difficult to compete with the railways which could offer reduced journey times and a greater degree of comfort. She was considered surplus to requirements in 1911 and was sold to foreign buyers who renamed her "Westerland". After several further changes of ownership she was scrapped at Genoa in 1925.

Southwold Beach Looking South Towards The Harbour

Published by F. Jenkins and postally used on July 28th 1906.

Notice the hive of activity on the beach with fishing boats and their gear competing for space with deck chairs and bathing machines. These machines belonged to Sam May whose name can just be seen painted on the hut in the foreground.

Card addressed to Miss. Elsie Dickinson in Highgate. The message is somewhat cryptic "Does this take your fancy?"

The popularity of sea bathing and the proliferation of bathing machines on the beach south of Gun Hill, had by August 1906, become a sufficiently pressing matter for the Town Council to debate the issues. There was a concern expressed that the nearer the machines got to the harbour so there was an increased risk to bathers' safety from treacherous currents around the harbour mouth.

The Town Council had already accepted the need for tents on the beach in front of the town both for propriety and for the convenience and use of bathers. Now they took the decision to allow bathing machines to be put there as well. Machines belonging to Mr. Herrington could be placed between East Cliff and the North Borough Boundary at a position to be selected by the Surveyor at a rate of 1/= per machine for the season.

<u>A Salutary Tale</u> – On August 22nd 1906 Mr. Geo. G. Crabbe of Finsbury Circus was charged with bathing in front of the Centre Cliff Hotel contrary to local by-laws. He had been seen in his bathing costume, accompanied by a lady, leave the Centre Cliff Hotel.

When warned by Insp. Ruffles that he was infringing local by-laws, he was heard to say "Give my compliments to the Mayor and tell him to go to h**l and to take his Corporation and by–laws with him!" Needless to say he was later found guilty and fined 10/=!

Damage Caused By High Tides January 1906

Damage caused by High Tides at Southwold, January, 1906.
East Cottages and Beach House in danger of falling

Publisher unknown. Postally used on March 8th 1906.

H. Molyneaux writes to Harry Paddison "One cannot walk in front of Beach House now. We do not think the groynes are doing any good."

In terms of storm damage to Southwold cliffs, 1906 had started badly with an exceptionally high tide on Tuesday January 16th combined with a strong SW wind which caused a major collapse of cliff in the area of South Cliff. This left a number of cottages in Primrose Alley in some danger. Some of the temporary piling in front of the Sailors' Reading Room was also wrecked.

Storm Damage To Southwold Cliffs March 13th 1906

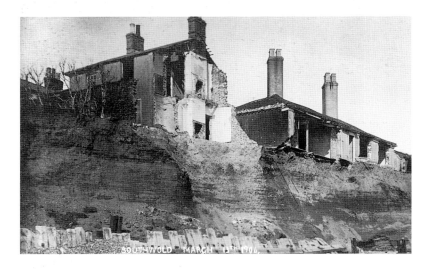

Published by F. Jenkins but not postally used.

Shows damage to Primrose Cottage and The Nook and gives some idea of the scale of the devastation sustained by property in this vicinity.

Gun Hill & South Beach March 13th 1906 Showing Storm Damage

Also published by F. Jenkins. Postally used on May 28th 1905.

The inland lake may be seen behind Gun Hill in the distance.

Another abnormally high tide combined with a heavy swell during the night of Monday March 12th caused more damage on an even greater scale than had previously been seen.

A large number of inhabitants were out to midnight and beyond watching the destruction. The Sailors' Reading Room was now only a matter of a few feet from the cliff edge and the flags in front had to be removed. Cliff House which had been used by fishermen as a lookout went down into the sea and at Beach House the cliff face was now sheer in line with the walls of that property.

The tide came over Gun Hill and left an inland lake on the marshes behind, where the wrecks of three fishermen's huts could be seen as well as a floating boat that had been carried over.

As might be expected at the Town Council meeting in April of that year, there was some discussion about the best way to protect the cliff against further inroads. It was eventually agreed to add a further 24 feet to the groyne in front of the Sailors' Reading Room as a precautionary measure. In May there were more worries expressed by Councillors about the state of the cliff especially as the Summer Season was about to start. It was agreed to purchase 20 piles and some pile driving equipment from the contractor E.A. Page whose estimate to do the job had been considered too high. The total cost of this gear from the contractor was £160.

The Wreck Of The Idun – January 17th 1912

WRECK OF THE "IDUN". SOUTHWOLD. JANY 17th 1912.

Publisher almost certainly F. Jenkins. Card not postally used.

Shows the 'Idun' being battered by waves on the beach and remarkably still in one piece despite the pounding.

A fierce easterly gale blew on January 17th 1912 and a call for a lifeboat was received at Southwold at about 6.40 p.m. concerning the Norwegian barque "Idun" which was in difficulties just off the beach. Earlier she had been picked up by the steam trawler "Adelaide" but the tow rope had broken and she had now come ashore opposite the lighthouse. The "Alfred Corry" lifeboat had already gone to the aid of another vessel, the "Voorwarts" which was in difficulties at Minsmere Sluice so the smaller lifeboat "Rescue" was dragged through the town and launched from its carriage near the pier. However, because of the tide, heavy sea and the shallow water, the "Rescue" was unable to get alongside.

Coast guards under the command of Chief Officer Davis on the beach fired five rockets over the craft but because of problems of communication with those on board it was some time before they were connected. Eventually, within 30 minutes of coming ashore a line was successfully attached and a breeches buoy got out. The first man was pulled ashore at 7.45 p.m. The rescue of the others was not without drama, as one man fell from the breeches buoy and into the surf as he came ashore. He was rescued by some of the crowd of onlookers who waded into the surf and pulled him to safety. The last man to come ashore was Capt. Christensen who was safely landed at 8.30 p.m.

The eight men and one boy were taken to The Shipwrecked Mariners Society at the Red Lion. The coast guards remained on duty throughout the night to deter any looting of the wreck.

The rescue was said to be one of the most exciting ever witnessed at Southwold, even the flares lit by the coast guards added an extra dimension to the unfolding drama by giving the wreck the ghostly appearance of a phantom ship.

In the following days and after the crew had removed all their personal property the barque was declared a total wreck. It was sold by Messrs. Hobsons on January 29th for £65.00 and then broken up where she lay on the beach.

The Crew Of The Idun — January 17th 1912

Publisher almost certainly F. Jenkins. Card not postally used.

Shows the crew of eight men and one boy pictured outside the Guardship on the cliff close to the site of the wreck.

DOWN THE
HARBOUR

Old Salt Works

OLD SALTWORKS, SOUTHWOLD.

Published by E.T.W.Dennis and postally used on the 18th February 1916.

T.B. writes to Mr. and Mrs. Womack at Dereham "If this was as convenient as Yarmouth and as cheap I would come up for a week-end. This is an awkward place to get at in or out." Some things do not seem to change!

The salt works were situated at the head of Salt Works Creek and were probably the last to operate in Suffolk.

Sea water was allowed in to the creek at high tide and given time to allow any solids to settle before being collected in the well at the head of the creek. When the condition of the water was judged to be at the right density for its purpose it was then pumped over Ferry Road to the salt pans on the other side via a long wooden trough. The windmill for this purpose may be clearly seen on the postcard. (There was also a small hand pump if there was insufficient wind for the mill to work.) The three salt pans can also be seen in the distance on the other side of the road. When the well had been emptied, the sluice at the seaward end of the creek was opened to allow more water in.

When the water reached the pans it was heated to boiling by coal fires to evaporate the water and so crystalise the salt. The hotter the fire the finer the salt. The coarse salt was mainly used in the local fishing industry and that of finer quality for domestic purposes.

Towards the end of the 19th Century and after nearly two centuries of a somewhat struggling existence, the salt works found it increasingly difficult to compete economically with salt now coming by rail from the large scale mining operations in Cheshire and eventually were closed in 1894. The plant and stock were sold off and the buildings, with the exception of the cottage were pulled down.

Southwold Harbour Reconstruction

Published by F. Jenkins and postally used on August 21st 1906.

Scene shows the first pile of the new harbour being sunk by the Countess of Stradbroke with other dignitaries and a large group of onlookers in attendance.

Message to Mrs. A. Waters in Halifax reads "Dear A. I thought you would like a copy of the "Red Letter Day" here. There were a great many people to witness the ceremony..."

The harbour by the 1890's was completely derelict. In 1898 a Board of Trade authority was obtained, abolishing the old Harbour Commissioners and vesting responsibility for the harbour in the Town Corporation. The Corporation then embarked on a scheme to save the harbour and capitalise on the increasing prosperity of the herring trade which brought up to 1000 Scottish boats south following the herring shoals causing severe congestion to the ports of Lowestoft and Great Yarmouth. Their aims were twofold: 1) to save the harbour 2) to boost the local economy.

In June 1906 the Corporation made a proposal to reconstruct the harbour and an application was made to the Board of Trade under the Southwold Harbour Order of 1898 to sell the harbour to a private company (Anthony Fasey & Sons Leytonstone) for redevelopment. The Board of Trade held a formal inquiry at Southwold Town Hall on 6th June 1906 and expressed enthusiasm for the project, though in effect the Corporation and the company had already come to a mutual agreement five days before the Board's formal inquiry. There was a ceremonial handing over of the keys to the harbour on 17th July 1906 when William Fasey paid half a guinea to the Mayor, Edgar Pipe. The cost of the redevelopment was estimated as being in the region of £65,000. The Board of Trade was prepared to make a grant of £15,000 towards the cost with Fasey & Sons finding the rest. The Board also agreed that the newly formed Southwold Harbour Company could lease land adjoining the proposed redevelopment at a rent of £1.00 per acre with an option to buy.

The scheme involved a considerable extension to the existing wooden piers with the North overlapping the South and bending them southwards at the outer ends to give some shelter from on-shore gales. The original length of the North pier was fixed at 250 feet. The Southwold side would contain all the things considered necessary for a fishing port of some significance such as gutting stations, pickling plots and market offices. The new quay walls would be made of concrete and bollards would be placed on the quay on the North side. The river would be dredged out up to the site of the ferry, with a depth of 12 feet at low water as far as Salt Works Creek (compared with between two and four feet as previously).

Work started in August 1906 with the ceremonial sinking of the first pile by Lady Stradbroke and the plan was to get the new harbour ready in time for the opening of the fishing season in the autumn of 1907 and compete with Lowestoft for the valuable Scottish fishing trade. Progress did not run as smoothly as expected. When the Company was advised at an early stage that the planned length of the North pier should be increased to 360 feet at an additional cost of £2,500, the Corporation was approached for £700. As the Corporation did not have this amount of money at their disposal they agreed instead to schedule an additional 27 acres of land on the same terms and conditions as before.

Considerable opposition to the whole scheme especially the surrender of more land belonging to the town now began to be expressed by some members of the Town Council, particularly Mr. Wrightson and Mr. Short. As a result, work on the project got badly behind schedule and the harbour was not opened until 1908. In the meantime there was considerable build up of sand around the North pier which spilled over to form a bar across the harbour mouth necessitating continual dredging.

In the first year of its operation, 296 boats visited the port landing over 6,000 tons of fish but the prosperity did not last. In 1909, although 761 boats used the harbour it was a poor fishing season with many gales. In the years immediately following, the number of boats using the harbour declined dramatically, possibly because of the increased capacity in the Hamilton Dock at Lowestoft. Another poor fishing season followed in 1911 and although 1912 and 1913 saw record landings at Yarmouth and Lowestoft, Southwold failed to prosper. Indifferent returns and lack of good rail links from the harbour had by this time undermined the early optimism that had followed the reconstruction. The Scottish boats did not come any more and the buyers and curers left.

Anthony Fasey & Sons had managed to save the harbour but not what was now left of the herring trade at Southwold. This was effectively killed off by the outbreak of war in 1914.

The harbour was bought back by the Corporation on 14th September 1931.

Southwold Harbour

Published by F. Jenkins and posted on October 25th 1908.

Mother writes to her daughter at the Bon Marche in Lowetoft "The Scotch boats have arrived and the girls are waiting to get to work. I think they have a nice lot of fish to start and now they have been once no doubt we shall see a lot more of them."

This view was taken on the Southwold side of the harbour looking across towards Walberswick. Masts abound in the river as well as one or two of the distinctive funnels of steam drifters. The distant white funnel belongs to the harbour tug "Pendennis." The quay side is stacked with barrels.

The Halesworth Times and Southwold General Advertiser of October 6th 1908 reported that the harbour "Now looks what it was made for." Business was beginning to take off. Thousands of barrels were piled on plots and salt was being stored in vast quantities as fast as it could be unloaded. The Scottish curers alone had sent between 6,000 and 7,000 barrels with each barrel destined to hold up to 800 herrings. Although no sign of them on this photograph, the first detachment of Scots girls had already arrived in town apparently causing a great deal of excitement in the Market Place before going on to their lodgings.

As most of the catch was destined for export to the Continent especially Russia, Spain, Germany and Italy, a new loop on the Southwold Railway had been built at Blythburgh Station to enable special goods trains with fish to pass the ordinary down traffic.

At this stage in its development it is estimated that about 100 persons were engaged on the shore at the harbour with activities connected in some way to the herring trade.

Packing Fish Southwold

Published by F. Jenkins. Not postally used.

Photograph shows Scots girls hard at work with an interested crowd of onlookers.

Walberswick and Ferry Southwold

Walberswick and Ferry, Southwold   Valentines Series 50858

Published by Valentines No.50858. Postally used on August 28th 1907.

Lillie writes to Mrs. Rouse in Ipswich as follows "We have had a day in Southwold. It was lovely. Picnic Thursday at the sluice..."

Before the formation of the River Blyth Ferry Company the crossing of the river was accomplished by open rowing boat, a method which had been employed since 1236.

In 1885 Sir John Ralph Blois, the franchise owner, granted the right to operate a ferry to H. J. Debney and E.M. Underhill Adnams who in turn assigned the lease to the recently formed River Blyth Ferry Company.

The company operated a manually operated pontoon on chains from bank to bank from a position midway between Blackshore Quay and the river mouth. Access was by ramp. Charges at the time of opening in 1885 were as follows:

Foot passengers 1½d.
Vehicles 3d.
Cattle 2d.
Sheep 1d.

The importance of the ferry at the time to both local inhabitants and visitors may be judged by the fact that in the first nine months of operation over 33,000 journeys were made by foot passengers alone and over 700 journeys by vehicles making the crossing.

The lack of any sort of aesthetic quality associated with the ferry meant that on looks alone it was always a butt for jokes and some guide books of the period were particularly scathing in their criticism of its appearance, calling it amongst other things "eye offending."

The pontoon became steam operated in 1899 at a cost of £111.00 and in 1927 it was replaced by another pontoon (built by John Chambers & Son Ltd. of Lowestoft).

The River Blyth Ferry Company ceased operations in February 1942. On closure, the ferry once again reverted to a rowing boat as now during the summer season.

Southwold Lifeboat

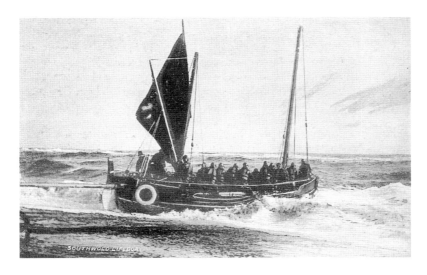

Published by F. Jenkins. Not postally used.

Southwold No. 1 lifeboat station was established in 1841 and the No. 2 station in 1866. During the fishing season one of the boats was always kept ready on the beach in case any emergency arose. Originally both lifeboat sheds were on the beach at a site roughly opposite the Ferry Road model yacht pond. As the beach suffered from periodic erosion and scouring making the launching and retrieval of the lifeboats difficult, the "Alfred Corry" was moved off the beach in 1908 and took up station in the river.

The "Rescue" shown in the postcard was the Southwold No. 2 lifeboat and was in service 1897 - 1920. As it was smaller and lighter than the "Alfred Corry" it was used mainly for inshore work. It was built in Lowestoft by Henry Reynolds who had premises in Commercial Road and on the south shore of the harbour there. The costs were met from a legacy from Mr. J. Barkworth. The design favoured, even though it was not self-righting, was known as the Norfolk and Suffolk type and relied on water ballast for stability. The Norfolk and Suffolk class lifeboats were the only sailing boats operated by the R.N.L.I. This was because the fishermen who crewed in them preferred a similar craft to their own sailing boats.

The "Rescue" was launched and christened by the wife of the late Mr. Barkworth on September 7th 1897. It was 32 feet long and 9 feet across the beam. It had room for 12 oars and a sail plan consisting of a lug fore sail and a standing lug mizzen. It was launched from a carriage, which meant that as it was a relatively light boat, it could be launched anywhere along the shore. This was necessary for instance when it went to the assistance of the "Idun" where it was towed through the town prior to launching so that it was able to get under the lee of the wreck. Similarly it could also be towed through the town on Lifeboat Day for fund raising purposes.

During its period on station it was launched eight times to assist with emergencies. There is some disagreement about the actual number of lives saved with a variety of figures between 15 and 23 quoted. On 19th April 1920 the No.2 station closed as it was felt there was no longer any need for a second lifeboat at Southwold. By this time too, the "Rescue" after being in service for 23 years, was considered beyond economic repair.

ACROSS THE
COMMON

The Common

"Wyndham" series No. W 7400. Postally used on August 10th 1910.

Cows graze contentedly. In the distance washing may be seen left on the gorse to dry.

Chris writes to Miss A. Aldridge in Leicester "This common is a lovely spot close to the golf links. We are having beautiful weather."

The extensive gorse fringed open space on the western side of the town is known as the Common and is the envy of many seaside towns though it is not common land. It was instead the gift of a wealthy Southwold merchant William Godyll, who in his will of 22nd May 1509 left it on trust to the inhabitants of Southwold in perpetuity to use as they so wished.

Until midway through the 19th Century the Common was mostly used for animal grazing though horse racing took place there between 1820 and 1834. Later on, the golf club became established on the Common in 1884. Organised sports and races were also introduced there on a regular basis in the early years of the 20th Century.

Over the years the function of the Common has continued to change and adjust to the needs of local people, to become what it is so greatly valued for today, a centre for recreation and quiet relaxation for all to enjoy as well as a haven for wildlife.

Golf Club House and Links

Golf Club House and Links, Southwold

Published by Valentines and postally used on May 8th 1914.

The clubhouse was opened in August 1894 after the committee agreed that the building and its erection should not cost more than £150.

L.M. Writes to Dr. Upward in Romford, "You'll like this place. We've had a motor run to Dunwich this morning."

Southwold Golf (and Quoit) Club was established in 1884. There were 16 original playing members who agreed that the entrance fee should be set at 5/= plus an annual subscription of 5/=. Honorary members paid one guinea and life members five guineas.

At the time of its formation there was only one other club in Suffolk and that was at Felixstowe. The newly formed club was granted permission by Southwold Corporation to play golf on the Common on February 4th 1884. The first clubhouse, basically no more than a wooden shed, was erected near the waterworks for the use and convenience of members.

The first round of golf on the new nine-hole course was played on 28th August 1884. The Halesworth & Southwold Almanack of 1894 observed that "One never thinks of Southwold without thinking of golf and the ever increasing popularity of the Links is capital evidence of their quality."

James Braid who went on to victory in five British Open Golf Championships between 1901 and 1910 was consulted in 1899 and again in 1900 about possible extensions to the course. James Braid's comment on the course was that "There are plenty of natural hazards without any requiring to be made".

There was some public concern expressed that the gorse recognised as one of the loveliest features of the Common would be sacrificed to the interests of sport. The Halesworth Times & Southwold General Advertiser claimed that "...for one who is attracted and pleased by golf one hundred will be delighted by the sight and smell of gorse blooms." However an accommodation was reached agreeable to all parties and a full 18-hole course was eventually opened in August 1904.

On The Golf Links

ON THE GOLF LINKS, SOUTHWOLD.

Published by J & S. Ltd. Not postally used.

Ladies playing golf on the 18 hole golf course after its establishment in 1904. The extended course was mostly built on marshland towards the harbour and Buss Creek. The current practice ground of the golf club occupies much of the land originally used for the opening three holes. Access to the next 7 holes which lay towards Buss Creek, was by a bridge over the Southwold Railway cutting. The remaining 8 holes were on the Common. The golf clubhouse, the water tower and St. Edmund's Church, which are all visible in the postcard, provide points of reference.

Southwold Sports 1907

Published by F. Jenkins Southwold. Unused.

In the card the canvas covered grandstand is clearly visible as well as what looks like the finish of the mile. The winner G. Hyde-Clarke (Unattached) won by ten yards from A. W. Fuller (Norfolk & Norwich A. C.)

Though there were Sports on the Common in 1879 to celebrate the opening of the Southwold Railway, regular Sports on the Common were first held there in 1902. They were organised under A. A. A. and N.C.U. rules. Meetings took place on Whit Monday and the event quickly established itself as one of the principal athletic meetings of East Anglia and attracted crowds of up to 2000. By 1907 an area of the Common was specifically set aside for the purpose complete with a canvas covered grandstand (the organisers had found to their cost that in previous years due to the size of the Common some spectators had been able to watch without paying). Admission was 1/= on the day or 6d if tickets were purchased beforehand.

The programme of events in athletics for 1907 included 120 yd., $\frac{1}{4}$, $\frac{1}{2}$ and one mile flat handicaps as well as a tug of war. There were two local winners: G. H. Court (Southwold F. C.) won the $\frac{1}{4}$ mile and J.H. Jillings (Southwold F. C.) the $\frac{1}{2}$ mile. Southwold Brewery finished runners up to Lowestoft Casuals in the tug of war. The team of C. Wilding, A. Upcraft, A. Smith, H. Button, G. Clow, C. Clow, G. Martin and G. Sagin each received prizes of postal orders for 2/6d.

In cycling there were one and two mile handicaps and a special attraction for 1907 was the Eastern Area N.C.U. Half Mile Championship.

The band of the 1st Norfolk Royal Garrison Artillery Volunteers entertained the crowd on the day.

Major Debney was one of the judges and Mr. R. J. Canova was the timekeeper.

Southwold Sports Motor Cycle Race May 27th 1912

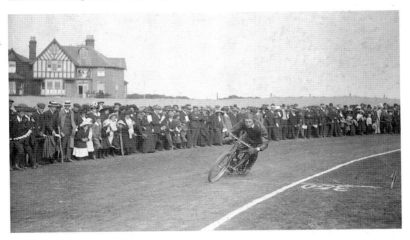

Publisher unknown and not postally used.

St. Barnabas is clearly visible in the background.

The tenth annual Southwold Sports were held on the Common under A. A. A. and N.C.U. rules on May 27th 1912. The weather was fine and there was a good crowd standing up to four or five deep to watch the racing. There was a great deal of interest, especially in the motor cycle racing as the track (as can be seen on the postcard) was none too wide. Health and safety issues were not a major consideration either for the riders or the spectators in those days! It must have required considerable skill, particularly on the corners, to get machines travelling at speeds up to 30 mph. safely round the course. Indeed, in its report on the event the local paper observed that "Once or twice machines bumped near the ropes while taking a wide turn at the tent end where the sightseers were thickly congregated."

Results of the Motor Cycling races:

TWO MILES   1) A.G. Miller   2 $^3/_4$. h.p. Humber
                         2) M. Matthew   3 $^1/_2$. h.p. Jap

Winners time 3min. 57 2/5.sec

FIVE MILES   1) W. Woods   3 $^1/_2$. h.p. Premier
                        2) S. Fryett   2 $^3/_4$. h.p. Royal Enfield

Winners time 10min. 8sec.

Mr. Norman C. Spratt Pictured In His 60 H.P. Deperdussin Anzani Monoplane

Publisher unknown but probably F. Jenkins. Not postally used.

Norman C. Spratt with his Deperdussin Monoplane.

Mr. Norman C. Spratt In Flight

FLYING AT SOUTHWOLD 60 HP DEPERDUSSIN MONOPLANE

Published by F. Jenkins. Not postally used.

The 11th Annual Sports on Whit Monday 1913 included an aeroplane flight from the Common as a special attraction. Aeroplaning by A.G. Miller was widely advertised in the local papers in the weeks before the Sports were held and obviously captured the imagination of the local inhabitants judging by the large number of spectators present on the day. The crowd of over 5,000 was more than double that of any previous occasion.

In glorious weather Mr. Norman C. Spratt of the British Deperdussin Monoplane Company attended in place of Mr. A. G. Miller whose monoplane had unfortunately been damaged whilst in transit through London.

In the morning Mr. Spratt took up five passengers and more passenger carrying flights had been planned to take place at the conclusion of the sports in the afternoon but unfortunately the elevator of his machine was broken by the crush of the crowd during the distribution of prizes. He did however manage a very successful solo effort during an interval in the sports in the afternoon. Despite the handicap of unfavourable wind conditions he gave a fine display to an enthusiastic crowd for between 10 and 15 minutes. He first of all flew west and returned to the Common via a circular route, which took him over the beach and the sea, reaching an altitude of 900 feet. He was loudly applauded on his safe return.

Duke of York's Camp

Publisher unknown. Postally used on 2nd August 1938.

The Duke of York's camp was held on the Common during the August Bank Holiday week between the years 1931 - 1938. The site of the camp was on the right hand side of the road leading to the harbour.

Moss writes to Bill at the Marine Parade Lowestoft "Just a card to let you know he is coming to camp on Tuesday."

George VI when Duke of York inaugurated a camp for boys who would be his guests for the August Bank Holiday each year. The first one was held in 1920 (though not at Southwold) and the boys who attended came from all walks of life and from all parts of the country. "Abandon Rank All Ye Who Enter Here" was the camp motto.

The great feature of the camps was a visit from the Duke of York himself. He would stay 24 hours with the boys and join in all the fun and games.

Between 1931 and 1938 the camp was held at Southwold largely through the initiative of Councillor Mrs. Hope who seeing in the national press that a new site was being sought persuaded the Council to offer the Common as a potential venue. The invitation was sent and duly accepted.

There was an exhaustive programme of activities from 7.30 a.m. to 10.30 p.m. Bugles sounded for meals (prepared by top chefs from Harrods and the Savoy Hotel) and for bathing times on the beach. There were morning and evening prayers and the boys themselves provided nightly entertainment.

Sunburn was a particular problem that frequently kept the camp doctor busy. However, nothing quite matched the hazard presented by hailstones the size of golf balls which fell on the camp in 1931!

The last camp held on the Common was in 1938 when the Royal Yacht "Victoria and Albert III" with the Royal Family on board anchored in Sole Bay en route to Scotland to allow the King as he now was to attend.

The Royal Yacht Off Southwold August 1938

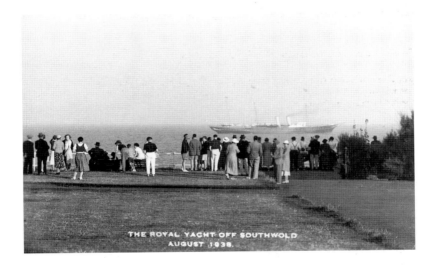

Published by F. Jenkins but not postally used.

The Royal Yacht "Victoria and Albert III" may be seen at anchor less than a mile from the shore.

AROUND THE TOWN

Market Place

Published by Jarrolds and postally used on August 18th 1906.

Bert sends cryptic message to Edith in Shepherds Bush "This bus goes from Southwold to Lowestoft."

The Market Place is triangular in shape and is approached via the High Street. From the Market Place, East Street leads towards the sea and Queen Street to South Green. Until the early years of the 19th century it contained a market cross which was pulled down in 1808. In 1873 Major Grubbe, Mayor of Southwold, erected a cast iron town pump in the Market Place. It is inscribed "Pro Bono Publico" and shows herrings (though they look like dolphins) and the crown and crossed arrows of St. Edmund. The pump was cast close by in the foundry owned by George Child in the yard off the Market Place still known as Child's Yard.

Southwold had been granted permission to hold a market every Thursday as early as 1220 and when the town became a town corporate by a Charter granted by Henry VII in 1490 it was allowed to hold a further market on Mondays.

The Market Place is the site of the Town Hall as well as a busy commercial centre for the town. For a time it was also the site of the town gaol.

Kelly's Directory for 1904 records the following businesses in the area:

Adnams & Co.	Swan Hotel	Market Place
John Aldred	Florist & Greengrocer	21, Market Place
Herbert Boggis	Butcher	23, Market Place
R. V. Britten	Dentist	13, Market Place
Capital & Counties Bank	Bank	Bank Ho. Market Place
Earnest R. Cooper	Solicitor	1, Market Place
Edwin Dale	Hairdresser & Tobacconist	5, Market Place
Denny & Sons	Tailors	11 & 13, Market Place
Thomas Denny	Grocer, Draper, Wine & Bottled Beer Retailer	2, Market Place
Walter Hanner	Chemist	15, Market Place
Charles Jacobs	Shoeing & General Smith	9, Market Place
T. Key	Architect & Surveyor	1, Market Place
William King	Cooper	7, Market Place
Stephen Reynolds	Grocer, Draper, Outfitter, Provision Merchant & House Agent	Market Place
Edgar Smith	Antique Dealer	19, Market Place
Stanford & Broom	Auctioneers	1, Market Place
William J. Waters	Baker, Pastry-Cook, Confectioner & Refreshment Rooms	8, Market Place

High Street Looking West

Published by F. Jenkins and postally used on 4th May 1920.

There is plenty of activity in the High Street in this postcard though few vehicles! F. Jenkins' shop on the right hand side of the street may be clearly seen. It has its awning out with a "Kodak" advertisement above it.

M. B. writes to The Rev. P. S. Douglas at Royston: "Have come here for the day to bring Cynthia back to school. We shall have done 140 miles by the time we get back. We have had three punctures and a burst tyre...!"

High Street Looking East

High Street From E. Southwold.

Published by Valentines No. 50857. Postally used, though stamp and postmark missing.

A. Tilbury writes from 27 Stradbroke Road to Mrs. Andrews in Andover "We arrived quite safe... Look after Ginger won't you"

The High Street is the main road into Southwold. Though there are a number of residential properties situated here, because it is the main road, it has always been important commercially, as the number of shops which are visible in the postcard suggest. The High Street leads on to what might be regarded as the commercial centre of Southwold situated around the Market Place.

Some idea of the scale and extent of the business life in the High Street in 1904 may be judged by the number of entries in the commercial section in Kelly's Directory for that year:

Herbert Adnams	Auctioneer & Estate Agent	76 High Street
Robert Allen	Builder & Insurance Agent	39 High Street
Barclays	Bank	High Street
Robert Blowers	Shoeing & General Smith	42 High Street
Edwin Bridge	Hairdresser & Fancy Repository	77 High Street
D. E. Canova	Watchmaker & Jeweller	73 High Street
Francis Carter	Paperhanger	78 High Street
Thomas W. Carter	Crown Hotel	High Street
John Chapman	Newsagent & Tobacconist	79 High Street
Jane Clarke	Baker & Confectioner	35 High Street
Robert Critten	Chemist	100 High Street
H.J. Debney & Sons	Grocers, Drapers, Wines & Spirits	37 High Street
Denny & Sons	Tailors	98 High Street
Minnie Denny	Girls School - Sutherland House	56 High Street
Frederick Easthaugh	Baker & Confectioner	64 High Street
Aaron Field	Antiques	57 & 59 High Street
Charles Field	Boot & Shoe Dealer	88 High Street
Robert Forrest	Post Office	High Street
David Francis	Machinist	63 High Street
James Fryett	Butcher	71 High Street
William Girling	Beer Retailer	2 High Street
Francis C. Goffin	Pork Butcher	21 High Street
Edward Goldsmith	Greengrocer	27 High Street
Donald Gooding	Insurance Agent	49 High Street
Edward Hall	Southwold Arms Public House	58 High Street
William Hammond	Dairyman	55 High Street
Alfred Howard	Decorator & Sanitary Plumber	75 High Street
Henry Hurr	Saddler	53 High Street
Frederick Jenkins	Photographer With Dark Room For Amateurs, Picture Framer, General Stationery, Artists Materials & Art China.	94 High Street
E.A. Juler	Watch & Clockmaker	82 High Street
Allan Manby	General & Furnishing Ironmonger	69 High Street
John Marshall	Kings Head Public House	High Street
Michael Pendrey	Ironmonger	66 High Street
William Stammers	Shopkeeper	25 High Street
Stead & Simpson Ltd	Boot & Shoemakers	74 High Street
James Waters	Grocer	18 High Street
Wright & Cox	Plumbers & House Decorators	6 High Street

Denny & Sons Tailors

Published by W.H. Smith and postally used on the 1ˢᵗ August 1911.

John writes to Mrs. Brown in Holloway "Dear Ma, We have just taken a trip here and like it much better than where we were."

Dennys an old and respected business in the town used to trade from this site now occupied by Somerfields. They were essentially ladies and gentlemen's tailors and general outfitters though interestingly their adverts for the time proclaim that genuine navy serge "as used by H.M. Government" was always kept in stock. They also specialised in clothing for boating, cycling and golf to accommodate the needs of the influx of summer visitors and when the need arose they could "re-cover umbrellas in a few minutes"!

Sir Alfred Munnings the artist, Adrian Bell the author and George Orwell were among their distinguished customers.

Motor Bus

Published by Valentines. Not postally used.

The vehicle in the picture is a 24h.p.Thorneycroft omnibus of about 1907.

The Great Eastern Railway Company started a motor omnibus service between Southwold and Lowestoft on Monday July 18th 1904. It was not, as one might suspect, a service primarily for visitors although the scenic beauty of the route was emphasised but for local people especially fishermen working out of Lowestoft and living in the villages south of the port.

Initially two buses were provided, each one making three journeys each way in the course of a day. The journey of approximately 12 miles took one hour and forty minutes with stops at Reydon, Wangford, Wrentham and Kessingland although passengers could be picked up and set down at any point along the route if necessary. Strangely, no luggage or bicycles were accepted on board although parcels up to 14 lb. were permitted as freight at a cost of 4d pre-paid. There were some minor irritations experienced by the early passengers such as the amount of dust thrown up off the road and for those riding on top, the overhanging branches of trees lining the road between Reydon and Southwold were a particular hazard.

The original buses were built by Milns-Daimler at a cost of £1,000 each and could accommodate 18 passengers on the outside and 16 inside. Two passengers could also sit by the side of the driver. Safety was a major consideration with three brakes being fitted. The drivers were fully qualified mechanics. Each bus carried a conductor and the fare for a single journey was 1/3d.

South Green

Published by F. Jenkins. Not postally used.

The flags that are visible in this postcard are part of the celebrations in the town to mark the coronation of George V in 1911.

Southwold House

Southwold House.

Published by A.H.J. and postally used on 20th January 1919.

Southwold House is a large marine villa dating from the 18th Century. It was extensively rebuilt in the 19th Century by Daniel Fulcher for Alfred Lillingstone (Mayor of Southwold 1852 - 1866). This building has long spikey window arches giving it a distinctive architectural style, which is rather different from those around it. It was the home of Augusta, Countess of Stradbroke for a time at the turn of the last century and later became a boarding house for St. Felix School.

On April 25th 1659 Southwold suffered a devastating fire. Fanned by a strong wind 238 dwellings were consumed within the space of four hours. The town hall, market place and gaol were also destroyed together with most of the commercial premises of the town. It has been suggested that 300 families may have suffered substantial losses with the overall bill running to £40,000. The distress was so great that Southwold was declared a disaster area by order of Parliament and a collection was made on behalf of those affected in every church in the land. This was probably the first national appeal for a disaster fund ever collected.

Southwold's Greens, of which South Green is the largest and probably the most attractive, date from this period and emerged as distinctive features of the town in the aftermath of the fire. When the rebuilding of the Borough began these areas were left as natural fire-breaks to prevent the town ever again being overwhelmed by such a disaster.

It was not until the 18th Century when sea bathing and seaside holidays were becoming popular that South Green began to attract the interest of the gentry. They could see the potential of South Green and the adjoining Gun Hill as an ideal site for their large and expensive marine villas. Substantial development in this respect was begun as early as 1807 with the construction of properties such as Stone House and Southwold House and continued throughout the century. There was also considerable speculative investment in the construction of elegant and superior lodging houses such as those that form the terrace at Centre Cliff to cater for the growing numbers of casual visitors who wanted to spend their holidays by the sea.

H. J. Debney & Sons

Published by S. M. Gibson. Not postally used.

Henry Johnson Debney's shop was situated on South Green in what is now known as the Homestead. It was established in 1816 and was the flagship store of an enterprise which at one time or another included shops at North Cliff on the corner of Chester Road with Stradbroke Road, 37 High Street and at Walberswick. Probably the nearest thing Southwold ever had that resembled a chain store at the time!

Essentially Debneys were grocers and wine and spirit merchants but their enterprises included house furnishings, drapery, millinery, dressmaking as well as running a house and estate agents business.

Chester Road

Chester Road, Southwold   Valentines Series   50868

Published by Valentines. Not postally used.

This view of Chester Road taken from the corner with Stradbroke Road shows Debney's shop on the left. Notice the goat cart outside the shop.

Stradbroke Road Looking Towards The Lighthouse

S.12115   STRADBROKE ROAD, SOUTHWOLD.

Published by W.H. Smith No. S.12115. Not postally used.

Shows Stradbroke Road looking south towards the lighthouse. The Victorian villas still have their decorative iron railings at the front. These were later removed so they could be melted down for armaments to help the war effort.

Originally called St. James' Street, Stradbroke Road was more than just a residential street in the early years of the 20th Century. It was both a commercial centre of some significance as well as an important location of properties offering holiday lodgings for summer visitors.

In Kelly's Directory for 1900 the following commercial premises are recorded:

No. 9	R.G. Simpson	Ironmonger
No. 10a	Wangford Dairy Supply	Milk, Butter, Cream, Eggs & Dressed Fowls
Frederick Ho.	R. Newson	Baker, Pastry-Cook & Confectioner
No. 11	H.J. Debney & Sons	Grocer, Draper & Wine & Spirits Merchant
No. 58	C. J. Andrews	Grocer & Post Office

Additionally, there was also a coal merchant, fish merchant and a builder living in the street at the time.

Apartments and Lodging Houses in Stradbroke Road:

No. 22	Mrs. J. Nolloth
No. 30	Mr. B. Brown.
No. 32	Mrs. E. Lamprill
No. 38	Mr. J. Hurr
No. 50	Mr. S. Powditch
No. 62	Mrs. E. Rice.
No. 66	Mrs. J. Rose

W. P. Gale of Halesworth published a Southwold Visitors List as a supplement to the Halesworth Times and Southwold General Advertiser every Friday during the summer season. It was in book form and cost one half penny.

Visitors staying in Stradbroke Road according to the list for August 17th 1900 came mainly from London and the suburbs. Other places of origin as diverse as Birkenhead and Rotherham were recorded. Some visitors as one might expect came from Norwich, Ipswich and Cambridge. Of the 80 or so properties in Stradbroke Road during that week 37 were shown as accommodating visitors.

Building Works In Stradbroke Road

Publisher unknown. Not postally used.

Shows a group of workmen outside what is believed to be No. 43 Stradbroke Road which is under construction, though the evidence is not conclusive.
(Could this be Wymering Road instead?)
Notice the wooden scaffolding poles and the "Sold" notice in the window.

St. Edmunds Church

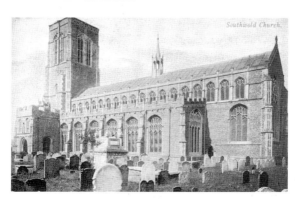

Published by Jarrolds. Not postally used.

This church is of great interest and beauty. It is 43m (144feet) long and 17m (56feet) wide. Notice the unfinished look of the massive tower and the delicate tracery of the windows.

SOUTHWOLD CHURCH

Southwold Church published by F. Jenkins. Not postally used.

Shows the very elegant south porch. This was probably added to the original building some 50 years after the main structure had been completed.

This magnificent Perpendicular church probably dates from the reign of Henry IV in the early years of the 15th century and was built on the site of a former chapel of ease dependent on Reydon church. Southwold before this time was little more than a hamlet and of much less importance than Reydon.

The exterior of the church is beautifully faced with flints. The two-storeyed porch is a slightly later addition to the church and has attractive flint chequer-boarding flushwork on both sides and richly panelled battlements. The canopied niche visible above the door now contains a statue of St. Edmund.

The impressive tower is 100 feet high and contains a peal of eight bells. The absence of any battlements or parapet suggest that the tower is unfinished, perhaps because the builders feared the foundations would not stand the weight. A Latin inscription "St. Edmund ora p nobis" set in stone above the west window, with a crown above each letter, asks St. Edmund to pray for us. Inside, the church is equally handsome from the proportion of the pillars and arches, to the height and beauty of the lofty ceiling and the delicate carvings, tracery and paintings of the rood screen.

Tree Planting Festival 1908

Published by F. Jenkins but not postally used.

This postcard commemorates the inaugural Arbor Day on November 20th 1908.

It has been suggested that the idea of an Arbor Day may have been a civic response to the perceived need for more trees in the town and its immediate environs where it was generally accepted, somewhat mistakenly, that trees did not flourish in a seaside environment. Arbor Day was started in 1908 with the planting of trees on

St. Edmund's Green opposite the hospital on 20th November,
St. Edmund's Day. The procession formed up in the Market Place
consisting of the Mayor (E.W. Moore) and the Corporation, the Vicar
(Rev. C. H. Sutton), the Boys' Brigade and members of the local Trade
Unions with their banners. Three trees were planted, one by the Mayor,
one by the Vicar and one by Mr. E. Pipe Chairman of the Trades Union.

Southwold Railway Locomotive

Published by F. Jenkins. Not postally used.

Shows No. 3 locomotive named "Blyth" at Southwold Station.

In the postcard from left to right:

Finch (Booking Clerk) against engine, J. Stannard (Driver) on footplate, F. C. Moore
(Fireman), Albert Self (W. Doy's dray driver), E. (Ted) Cox (Porter/ Shunter),
Case (Lad Porter), Walter Calver (Station Master 1900 - 1908), E. (Ted) Bailey
(Goods Porter) under tree with bicycle.

Southwold Railway Station

THE STATION, SOUTHWOLD

Published by H. C. Buckler. Not postally used.

Shows Southwold Railway Station and the Station Hotel (now renamed the "Blyth").

After previous failed attempts, finally in 1875 there was general agreement among local people that the prosperity of the area would be enhanced by connecting Southwold to the Great Eastern line at Halesworth.

Two public meetings were held in October of that year, one at Halesworth with Mr. Charles Easton of Easton Hall in the chair and one at Southwold under the chairmanship of the Earl of Stradbroke. The meetings were addressed by Mr. A. Pain an engineer who had extensive experience of light railways and whose idea was to build a railway of 2 ft. 6 in. gauge which he claimed would reduce overall costs and maintenance compared with standard gauge.

The active interest and support of large local landowners like these gave the project necessary impetus. Capital of £68,000 was raised through debentures, preference and ordinary shares. The Southwold Railway Act was passed in 1876 and despite worries about the necessary finance being forthcoming the railway duly opened to the public on September 24th 1879 with some modifications to the original plan, notably an increased gauge of 3 feet. Thomas Jellicoe was the first secretary of the

Company and the aforesaid Arthur Pain became the manager and chief engineer.

The route was along the Blyth valley passing through the villages of Holton, Wenhaston (station opened Sept.1879) Blythburgh, (station opened Dec.1879) and Walberswick, (station opened Sept.1882) crossing the river by means of an iron swing bridge before terminating in Southwold. The total distance was about 8 3/4 miles. The fare on opening was 1/6d first-class and 9d third-class.

Initially there were three locomotives all built by Sharp Stewart & Co. Ltd. They were numbered and named as follows: No.1 Southwold, No.2 Halesworth and No.3 Blyth. The Board of Trade imposed a speed restriction of 16 mph. and the total journey time was about 35 minutes. Passengers were carried in 6 wheeled coaches built to a tramcar pattern with a veranda and door at each end. Each coach could accommodate about 40 passengers seated facing each other. First class passengers had cushions on the wooden seats, third class had a strip of carpet. Heating for first class was by hot water foot warmers while third class had straw ankle deep on the floor. Lighting was by oil lamps.

Business was slow to start with and although trade did pick up in the nineties it was not until 1910 that the company was able to pay a dividend to its Ordinary shareholders. At the height of its prosperity between 1912 and 1913 the railway was carrying 100,000 passengers a year and helping to lay the foundations that were to make Southwold a popular summer resort. However trade did not recover after the First World War and the increased competition from mechanised road transport eventually sounded the death knell for the so-called "toy railway." The railway closed on 11th April 1929.

The Railway That Never Was!

On the 24th December1900, the Light Railway Commissioners held an inquiry at Southwold Town Hall to consider two major proposals brought by the Southwold Railway Company. Firstly, to extend their line beyond Southwold to Kessingland and make it standard gauge at a cost of £48,000.00. Secondly, to widen the narrow gauge on their existing section from Halesworth to Southwold to match the standard gauge of 4 feet 8 1/2 inches at an estimated cost of £36,000.00.

The proposals envisaged a station at Reydon (which would also serve Wangford), a siding at South Cove for the brickworks and general goods traffic, with further stations at Wrentham, Henstead and Kessingland where the line would join up with the Great Eastern network. The proposals were approved by the local inquiry and an Order was submitted to the Board of Trade on 23rd July 1901 which was duly approved with work to be completed by 1907.

There was considerable opposition to the scheme expressed by the Corporation of Southwold at the time. The major stumbling block was that members were not entirely convinced that the Company had the necessary funds or the wherewithal to raise sufficient capital. The Gooch family at Benacre Hall over whose land much of the route was planned was approached for financial help but declined though they did promise that they would sell the land at a favourable rate to the Company. There were also some practical difficulties too concerning level crossings.

With insufficient capital left after the rebuilding of all the road bridges on the existing line as well as the swing bridge over the river Blyth and without the support of the town council the proposals were subsequently shelved.

St. Felix School

A view of St. Felix School published by W.H. Smith. Postally used but stamp removed.

Girls From St. Felix On The Common

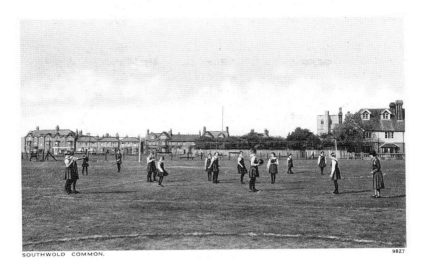

SOUTHWOLD COMMON.   9827

Published by J. Salmon. Not postally used.

Shows St. Felix girls from the Junior School having a games lesson on the Common.

St. Felix School was founded by Margaret Isabella Gardiner in 1897 when she moved here from Aldeburgh and started her school on premises around South Green. School House was established in the Golf Links Hotel (now Regency House). Gorse View (now part of St. Barnabas), Southwold House on South Green and Blyth House on St. James Green all became boarding houses. Two further properties on North Parade, Uplands and Dunburgh (then called Glan-y-don) also became boarding houses. The Elms (now May Place) became Miss. Gardiner's own home.

H.J. Debney & Sons on South Green were the stockists for the school uniform and the school hired the large dining room in the Centre Cliff Hotel for their important functions. Games were played nearby on the Common. When Trinity Fair was on, it was of course difficult to work in school on South Green so Miss. Gardiner solved the problem pragmatically by giving the girls a holiday and taking them out for picnics each day.

Meanwhile in 1900 building began on the present site on Halesworth Road and the school was able to move to the new buildings in 1902.

Miss Gardiner resigned through ill health in 1908 and was succeeded as head mistress by Miss. Lucy Silcox. The appointment of Miss. Silcox coincided with a rapid expansion of the number of pupils on roll.

In 1919 Miss. Silcox persuaded the School Governing Council to buy Centre Cliff Hotel and to convert it for use as a junior school. Once again girls took their games lessons on the Common. Centre Cliff remained the Junior School until 1940 when St. Felix was evacuated to Hinton St. George in Somerset.

BACK ALONG
THE SEA FRONT

Gun Hill

Published by Valentines in their "Carbotype" series No.86360. Not postally used.

Gun Hill so named because of the battery of six muzzle-loading Tudor cannon that had been placed there in 1746 after the Board of Ordnance had given them to the town. A more romantic story is that these cannon were ones that had originally been captured by "Bonnie Prince Charlie" at the battle of Prestonpans in 1745. They were said to have been recaptured by the Duke of Cumberland at Culloden later the same year and then presented by him to the town, supposedly as a gift for the enthusiastic reception given to him by the inhabitants of the town on his way back from Inverness. They were last fired on November 9th 1842 to celebrate the birthday of the Prince of Wales. The gun crews on that occasion were volunteer Coast Guards. One unfortunate gunner among them named James Martin lost his life when one of the guns held fire and went off at the very moment he was looking down the barrel to ascertain what the problem was.

Gun Hill And Beach

Published by F. Jenkins. Not postally used.

Shows Sam May standing in front of his hut. Sam served as First Coxswain on the "Alfred Corry" from 1898 until his retirement through ill health in 1918. He received medals from the French government and the Queen of Holland for daring rescues he carried out off the Suffolk coast. It was said that in 27 years service with the Southwold lifeboats he never failed to get them to sea and became something of a legendary figure on the beach in his own lifetime.

The Casino may be seen on the Hill.

This is a picturesque part of the town and a favoured place for holidaymakers to promenade and take in both the sea air and the views. An octagonal building known as the Casino was built there in 1810 as a subscription reading room with a comprehensive selection of newspapers and periodicals available to subscribers.

Southwold Lighthouse

The Lighthouse, Southwold.

Published by Chester Vaughan and postally used on September 6th 1907.

Edith writes to Mrs. Merrels at Chediston, "Dear Sarah- Received the box of eggs quite safe but you did not send the key. Can you send it in a letter...?"

Southwold lighthouse is somewhat unusual in that it stands almost in the centre of the town. It is a prominent landmark for passing shipping as well as a guide for vessels wishing to enter Southwold Harbour.

Construction began in 1887 under the supervision of Sir James Douglas, Engineer in Chief to Trinity House. It was built to a design by James Walker who had been responsible for other lighthouses along the East Coast at Cromer and Hunstanton. The cylindrical tower stands to a height of 101 feet on East Cliff which gives it an imposing overall height of approximately 120 feet above sea level.

The lighthouse was lit for the first time on 3rd September 1890. The light originally powered by an Argand oil burner was replaced by a Matthews incandescent burner in 1906. A Hood 100mm petrol burner was installed in 1923 and was in use until the lighthouse was electrified in 1938 with a 1,500 watt lamp. The present character of the light is group flashing four every 20 seconds. The lamp is visible for up to 17 miles with red sectors marking the dangerous Sizewell Sands to the south and the Barnard Sands to the north. The main navigation light is white.

The lighthouse has been unmanned since electrification in 1938.

Unemployed Workers Protest March At North Parade - January 25th 1907

Published by F. Jenkins. Postally used on February 15th 1907.

Card shows men laid off at the Harbour Works on January 24th 1907 making their way along North Parade to Councillor Short's residence in Corporation Road (now called Marlborough Road) to request that he withdraw his opposition to the reconstruction work going on at the harbour.

Work practically stopped on the Harbour Reconstruction Works on January 24th 1907 and the workers were sent home, principally because of the opposition to the scheme from two members of the Town Council, Mr. Wrightson and Mr. Short. The contractors Anthony Fasey Ltd. had previously written to the Council explaining that the continued opposition being expressed to the Harbour Order from the Council was frustrating the project and putting in jeopardy a substantial grant of £15,000 from the Board of Trade on which the whole project depended.

The 100 men or so affected by the lay-off together with sympathetic townspeople assembled in front of Mr. Wrightson's residence at Sea Croft, East Cliff and called upon him to withdraw his opposition. He came to the front of his home and addressed the gathering but declined to withdraw. The following evening, January 25th a number of men employed on the works again visited Councillor Wrightson and also Councillor Short who lived in apartments in Corporation Road but with little success in getting them to change their minds.

The matter was finally settled after a lengthy delay.

William Short later wrote to the local paper explaining his position. His main objection was that the Council was disposing of land belonging to the townspeople and selling it to a speculating company at a knock-down price. He wanted the proceeds of any land sold to be used to buy more land rather than be spent on what he considered to be an ill-conceived scheme for both harbour and sea defence.

Marlborough Hotel

Published by Jarrolds. Postally used Dec.29th 1909.

A.M. Buckingham writes to Mrs. Martin in Station Road Southwold and sends "Kind Xmas greetings. I hope you will have a very prosperous New Year and that all the family will have good health."

The Marlborough Hotel opened on April 3rd 1900 under the management of Mr. Carl Bennewitz. The architect for the enterprise was Arthur Pells F.S.I. of Beccles and Messrs. S. Howard & Sons Builders from Halesworth were given the contract.

The hotel occupied a fine position on the sea front at the corner of Dunwich and Corporation (later renamed Marlborough) Roads. It was built of red and moulded brickwork on three storeys with an octagonal turret and large bay windows and balconies. The landings and corridors were cleverly arranged on each floor in the same way so that sea views were obtainable from nearly all the 50 bedrooms. It proudly advertised "Bathrooms on each floor." It was furnished throughout by Maples of Tottenham Court Road London.

This hotel was keen to extend its summer season as it advertised itself as a pleasant winter residence "warmed by an elaborate system of radiators" to provide every home comfort.

However, just six years after it opened it was offered for sale at auction but there was little interest and it was withdrawn at £7,400.

The Marlborough Hotel was destroyed during the Second World War by a direct hit in a bombing raid on 15th May 1943.

Grand Hotel

Published by Woodstone-Barton in their "Milton " Series. Not postally used.

This postcard shows the imposing front elevation of the hotel. All that now remains is the low brick wall.

The Grand Hotel was completed in 1902 and at the time of construction was regarded as one of the finest hotels on the East Coast. It was built by the Coast Development Company to cater for visitors mostly arriving by steamer or train. The hotel stood on a prime site facing the sea with accommodation providing about 70 bedrooms as well as all the day rooms one might expect of a hotel of this size and class. It was regarded as an extremely modern and luxurious hotel at the time and much was made of the fact that it was lighted by electricity. The total cost of the completed hotel was something approaching £20,000.

The hotel was requisitioned by the Army during the Second World War and fell into disrepair. It was partially demolished for conversion into flats after the war but was eventually pulled down in 1959 and the site redeveloped with modern bungalows.

Published by Woodstone-Barton in their "Milton " Series. Not postally used.

This postcard shows the Vita sun lounge in the hotel and gives some indication of the style and quality of the furnishings of the interior.

Southwold Model Yacht Regatta August 10th 1907

Published by F. Jenkins. Not postally used.

Southwold still has two model yacht ponds, one at Ferry Road and one near the pier. The Ferry Road pond was provided by the Corporation and was free whereas there was a charge of 1d at the other one. This pond had been constructed by the Coast Development Company as part of the leisure complex associated with the development of the pier. Both ponds held regattas.

The postcard shows plenty of activity on the first day of the annual August regatta for model yachts in 1907. The Halesworth Times & Southwold General Advertiser reported favourable conditions of wind and weather at the Coast Development Company's pond near the pier. The Pier Master Mr. F. Usher assisted in the organisation and a crowd of about 200 was present to watch the racing.

AND TO FINISH WITH ...

SOME GENTLE SEASIDE HUMOUR

Published by F. Jenkins from the "Punch" Series but not postally used.

Artist C. Keene.

CHATTY VISITOR " SO THERES TOO MUCH WIND TO GO OFF TODAY. HOW DO YOU KNOW WHEN THE WIND IS RIGHT ?
TOM PALMER " WELL SIR. WE WATCH THE SMOKE FROM THE STEAMBOATS & IF IT BLOWS AWAY WE KNOW ITS
TOO WINDY - & IF IT GOES UP STRAIGHT THERES NOT ENOUGH "

Published and drawn by Reg Carter from "The Sorrows Of Southwold" Series One. Not postally used but originally drawn about 1916.

Reg Carter was a Southwold born artist with a studio beside Bank Alley. Local firms and characters were often included in his cartoons and are easily recognisable!

ACKNOWLEDGEMENTS

I would like to acknowledge the help and encouragement given to me in particular by Rachel Lawrence who kindly read the text of the draft manuscript and offered constructive criticisms and invaluable advice. Also to David Lee who lent his extensive knowledge of the local history of the area to the work and the practical and helpful suggestions he was able to make.

To Ann Thornton for her enthusiasm for the project and for allowing me to use the postcards originally published by her grandfather Frederick Jenkins. To Jarrolds Publishing for allowing me to reproduce the postcards on pages 37, 50 and 64. To J. Salmon Ltd. for permission to reproduce their postcard on page 57. Also to W.H. Smith for permission to use their postcards on pages 42, 48 and 56. Whilst every effort has been made to contact the publishers of other postcards used in this book it has not always been possible to do so for a variety of reasons. Therefore all the postcards used are credited with the name of the publisher where it is known and permission is respectfully requested, albeit retrospectively.

To Ros McDermott for her interest and advice.

Thanks also to the staff at the Suffolk Record Office at Lowestoft library.

This book makes no pretensions to be exhaustive. Any errors it may contain, or omissions, are the sole responsibility of the author and as such, I can only make a full and profound apology to the reader in advance, should this be the case.

Finally to my wife Ann for all the interest she has shown and her help and encouragement along the way without which this book could not have been produced.

NOTES